Made in the USA
Middletown, DE
05 May 2022

65359497R00071